To Peter
from
Dad + Mom
Happy 18th Biirthday
7-7-77

YOU
CAN
SEE
FOREVER

YOU
CAN
SEE
FOREVER

Compiled by Caesar Johnson

The C. R. Gibson Company
Norwalk, Connecticut

TABLE OF CONTENTS

WHO AM I?

The trees ask me,
And the sky,
And the sea asks me
    Who am I?

The grass asks me,
And the sand,
And the rocks ask me
    Who am I?

The wind tells me
At nightfall,
And the rain tells me
    Someone small.

    Someone small
    Someone small
      But a piece
        of
        it
        all.

FELICE HOLMAN

So for a moment I stand, my feet
   planted firm in the present,
Eagerly scanning the future which
   is so soon to possess me.
AMY LOWELL

I Am

You cannot dream yourself into a character; you must hammer and forge yourself one.
JAMES A. FROUDE

It ain't no disgrace for a man to fall; but to lay there and grunt is.
JOSH BILLINGS

You are today where your thoughts have brought you; you will be tomorrow where your thoughts take you.
JAMES ALLEN

Do not wish to be anything but what you are, and try to be that perfectly.
ST. FRANCIS DE SALES

If we are not responsible for the thoughts that pass our doors, we, at least, are responsible for those which we admit and entertain.
CHARLES B. NEWCOMB

A man said to the universe:
"Sir, I exist!"
"However," replied the universe,
"The fact has not created in me
A sense of obligation."
STEPHEN CRANE

There is in every man something greater than he had begun to dream of. Men are nobler than they think themselves.
PHILLIPS BROOKS

It is only imperfection that complains of what is imperfect. The more perfect we are, the more gentle and quiet we become towards the defects of others.
JOSEPH ADDISON

Had I to carve an inscription on my tombstone I would ask for none other than "The Individual."
SØREN KIERKEGAARD

Reputation is in itself only a farthing candle, of a wavering and uncertain flame, and easily blown out, but it is the light by which the world looks for and finds merit.
JAMES RUSSELL LOWELL

How majestic is naturalness. I have never met a man whom I really consider a great man who was not always natural and simple. Affectation is inevitably the mark of one not sure of himself.
CHARLES DAWES

Man is but a reed—the weakest thing in nature—but he is a reed that thinks. It is not necessary that the whole universe should arm itself to crush him. A vapor, a drop of water, is enough to kill him. But if the universe should crush him, man would still be nobler than that which slays him, for he knows that he dies; but of the advantage which it has over him the universe knows nothing. Our dignity consists, then, wholly in thought. Our elevation must come from this, not from space and time, which we cannot fill. Let us, then, labor to think well: that is the fundamental principle of morals.
BLAISE PASCAL

What happens to a man is less significant than what happens within him.

LOUIS L. MANN

A man has to live with himself, and he should see to it that he always has good company.

CHARLES EVANS HUGHES

The wind that fills my sails
Propels; but I am helmsman.

GEORGE MEREDITH

Life does not consist mainly—or even largely—of facts and happenings. It consists mainly of the storm of thoughts that is forever blowing through one's head.

MARK TWAIN

Who steals my purse steals trash; 'tis something, nothing;
'Twas mine, 'tis his, and has been slave to thousands;
But he that filches from me my good name
Robs me of that which not enriches him
And makes me poor indeed.

WILLIAM SHAKESPEARE

It is a fine thing to be honest, but it is also very important to be right.

WINSTON CHURCHILL

Maturity, we now know, need be no dull routine of a defeated and resigned adulthood. It can rather be the triumphant use of powers that all through our childhood and youth have been in preparation.

HARRY A. OVERSTREET

Character is like a tree, and reputation like its shadow. The shadow is what we think of it; the tree is the real thing.
ABRAHAM LINCOLN

I am only one, but I am one. I cannot do everything, but I can do something. And I will not let what I cannot do interfere with what I can do.
EDWARD EVERETT HALE

Don't bother just to be better than your contemporaries or predecessors. Try to be better than yourself.
WILLIAM FAULKNER

When a man gets talking about himself, he seldom fails to be eloquent and often reaches the sublime.
JOSH BILLINGS

It is the mind that maketh good or ill, that maketh wretch or happy, rich or poor.
EDMUND SPENSER

Who has deceived thee so often as thyself?
BENJAMIN FRANKLIN

Make the best use of what is in your power, and take the rest as it happens.
EPICTETUS

Life consists of what a man is thinking of all day.
RALPH WALDO EMERSON

The world is a looking glass, and gives back to every man the reflection of his own face.
WILLIAM THACKERAY

What lies behind us and what lies before us are tiny matters compared to what lies within us.
WILLIAM MORROW

Therefore am I still
A lover of the meadows and the woods,
And mountains; and of all that we behold
From this green earth; of all the mighty world
Of eye, and ear—both what they half create,
And what perceive; well pleased to recognize
In nature and the language of the sense
The anchor of my purest thoughts. . . .
WILLIAM WORDSWORTH

For the human mind is seldom at stay: If you do not grow better, you will most undoubtedly grow worse.
SAMUEL RICHARDSON

Better keep yourself clean and bright; you are the window through which you must see the world.
GEORGE BERNARD SHAW

A sense of humor is a sense of proportion.
KAHLIL GIBRAN

All that we are is the result of what we have thought. The mind is everything. What we think, we become.
BUDDHA

I have often thought that the best way to define a man's character would be to seek out the particular mental or moral attitude in which, when it came upon him, he felt most deeply and intensely active and alive. At such moments there is a voice inside which speaks and says: "This is the real me!"
WILLIAM JAMES

Let everyone be himself, and not try to be someone else. Let us not torment each other because we are not all alike, but believe that God knew best what he was doing in making us so different. So will the best harmony come out of seeming discords, the best affection out of differences, the best life out of struggle, and the best work will be done when each does his own work, and lets everyone else do and be what God made him for.
JAMES FREEMAN CLARKE

The man who has not anything to boast of but his illustrious ancestors is like a potato—the only good belonging to him is underground.
SIR THOMAS OVERBURY

You grow up the day you have your first real laugh—at yourself.
ETHEL BARRYMORE

Beauty is only skin deep, but it's a valuable asset if you're poor and haven't any sense.
KIN HUBBARD

Human beings are not born with human nature—they develop it.
ASHLEY MONTAGU

14 Make the most of yourself, for that is all there is of
you.
RALPH WALDO EMERSON

You gain strength, courage, and confidence by every
experience in which you really stop to look fear in the
face. You are able to say to yourself, "I lived through
this horror. I can take the next thing that comes along."
The danger lies in refusing to face the fear, in not
daring to come to grips with it. If you fail anywhere
along the line it will take away your confidence. You
must make yourself succeed every time. *You must do the
thing you think you cannot do.*
ELEANOR ROOSEVELT

I asked God for strength, that I might achieve,
   I was made weak, that I might learn
   humbly to obey . . .
I asked for health, that I might do greater things,
   I was given infirmity, that I might do
   better things . . .
I asked for riches, that I might be happy,
   I was given poverty, that I might be wise . . .
I asked for power, that I might have the praise of men,
   I was given weakness, that I might feel
   the need of God . . .
I asked for all things, that I might enjoy life,
   I was given life, that I might enjoy all things.
I got nothing that I asked for, but everything I had
   hoped for,
Almost despite myself, my unspoken prayers
   were answered,
I am among all men, most richly blessed.
UNKNOWN SOLDIER AT GETTYSBURG

| ODE

We are the music-makers,
    And we are the dreamers of dreams,
Wandering by lone sea-breakers,
    And sitting by desolate streams;
World-losers and world-forsakers,
    On whom the pale moon gleams:
Yet we are the movers and shakers
    Of the world for ever, it seems.

With wonderful deathless ditties
We build up the world's great cities,
    And out of a fabulous story
    We fashion an empire's glory:
One man with a dream, at pleasure,
    Shall go forth and conquer a crown;
And three with a new song's measure
    Can trample an empire down.

We, in the ages lying
    In the buried past of the earth,
Built Nineveh with our sighing,
    And Babel itself with our mirth;
And o'erthrew them with prophesying
    To the old of the new world's worth;
For each age is a dream that is dying,
    Or one that is coming to birth.

ARTHUR O'SHAUGHNESSY

GIVE ME THE SPLENDID SILENT SUN

Give me the splendid silent sun with all
    its beams full-dazzling,
Give me juicy autumnal fruit ripe and red
    from the orchard,
Give me a field where the unmowed grass
        grows;
Give me an arbor, give me the trellised
        grape,
Give me fresh corn and wheat, give me serene-
    moving animals teaching content.
Give me nights perfectly quiet as on high
    plateaus west of the Mississippi, and
    I am looking up at the stars,
Give me odorous at sunrise a garden of
    beautiful flowers where I can walk
        undisturbed.

WALT WHITMAN

The greatest discovery of my generation is that human beings can alter their lives by altering their attitudes.
WILLIAM JAMES

DAYS

Some days my thoughts are just cocoons—all
  cold, and dull, and blind,
They hang from dripping branches in the grey
  woods of my mind;

And other days they drift and shine—such
  free and flying things!
I find the gold-dust in my hair, left by
  their brushing wings.
KARLE WILSON BAKER

No life is so hard that you can't make it easier by the way you take it.
ELLEN GLASGOW

A man must seek his happiness and inward peace from objects which cannot be taken away from him.
ALEXANDER HUMBOLDT

Nothing in life is to be feared. It is only to be understood.
MARIE CURIE

I Feel

Joy and woe are woven fine,
A clothing for a soul divine:
Under every grief and pine
Runs a joy with silken twine.
It is right it should be so:
Man was made for joy and woe;
And when this we rightly know
Safely through the world we go.

WILLIAM BLAKE

Make peace with yourself, and heaven and earth will make peace with you. Endeavour to enter into your own inner cell, and you will see the heavens; because the one and the other are one and the same, and when you enter one you see the two.

ST. ISAAK OF SYRIA

Do not put off until tomorrow what can be enjoyed today.

JOSH BILLINGS

Sometimes when I'm lonely,
Don't know why,
Keep thinkin' I won't be lonely
By and by.

LANGSTON HUGHES

If we cannot live so as to be happy, let us at least so live as to deserve happiness.

JOHANN GOTTLIEB FICHTE

In all ranks of life the human heart yearns for the beautiful; and the beautiful things that God makes are His gift to all alike.

HARRIET BEECHER STOWE

21

In the midst of winter, I finally learned that there was in me an invincible summer.
ALBERT CAMUS

Sitting in silence,
Waiting for things to happen!
There's something in silence,
Waiting for things to happen,
    That gathers drama.
Maybe a leaf falls,
Or a raindrop will deepen
The tint of a stone:
A honeybee stumbles
Among foxglove stalls.
A proud spirit humbles
Itself to this humour;
The life of the sod,
The root, the sky,
The quietly known
Presence of God.
RICHARD CHURCH

If all the World looks drear, perhaps
    the meaning
Is that your windows need a little
    cleaning.
ARTHUR GUITERMAN

I remember my youth and the feeling that will never come back any more—the feeling that I could last forever, outlast the sea, the earth, and all men.
JOSEPH CONRAD

THE HIGH SCHOOL BAND

On warm days in September the high school band
Is up with the birds and marches along our street,
Boom, boom,
To a field where it goes boom boom until eight forty-five
When it marches, as in the old rhyme, back, boom boom,
To its study halls, leaving our street
Empty except for the leaves that descend, to no drum,
And lie still.
In September
A great many high school bands beat a great many drums,
And the silences after their partings are very deep.
REED WHITTEMORE

Life is like music; it must be composed by ear, feeling,
and instinct, not by rule.
SAMUEL BUTLER

It is the little bits of things that fret and worry us; we
can dodge an elephant, but we can't a fly.
JOSH BILLINGS

Misfortunes one can endure—they come from outside,
they are accidents. But to suffer for one's own
faults—ah!—there is the sting of life.
OSCAR WILDE

If the day and the night are such that you greet them
with joy, and life emits a fragrance like flowers and
sweet-scented herbs, is more elastic, more starry, more
immortal,—that is your success.
HENRY DAVID THOREAU

Change is an easy panacea. It takes character to stay in one place and be happy there.
ELIZABETH CLARKE DUNN

Happiness is a habit—cultivate it.
ELBERT HUBBARD

A pessimist is one who feels bad when he feels good for fear he'll feel worse when he feels better.
UNKNOWN

AFTER THE DENTIST

My left upper
lip and half

my nose is gone.
I drink my coffee

on the right from
a warped cup

whose left lip dips.
My cigarette's

thick as a finger.
Somebody else's.

I put lip-
stick on a cloth-

stuffed doll's
face that's

surprised when one
side smiles.
MAY SWENSON

To be interested in the changing seasons is a happier state of mind than to be hopelessly in love with spring.
GEORGE SANTAYANA

The art of living does not consist in preserving and clinging to a particular mood of happiness, but in allowing happiness to change its form without being disappointed by the change; for happiness, like a child, must be allowed to grow up.
CHARLES MORGAN

The greatest devotion, greater than learning and praying, consists in accepting the world exactly as it happens to be.
HASIDIC SAYING

Sunshine is delicious, rain is refreshing, wind braces up, snow is exhilarating; there is no such thing as bad weather, only different kinds of weather.
JOHN RUSKIN

A greater poverty than that caused by money is the poverty of unawareness . . . Men and women go about the world unaware of the goodness, the beauty, the glories in it. Their souls are poor. It is better to have a poor pocketbook than to suffer from a poor soul.
THOMAS DREIER

Lack of something to feel important about is almost the greatest tragedy a man may have.
ARTHUR E. MORGAN

Life leaps like a geyser for those who drill through the rock of inertia.
DR. ALEXIS CARREL

It is within the experience of everyone that when pleasure and pain reach a certain intensity they are indistinguishable.

ARNOLD BENNETT

Emotion is not something shameful, subordinate, second-rate; it is a supremely valid phase of humanity at its noblest and most mature.

JOSHUA LOTH LIEBMAN

Very little is needed to make a happy life. It is all within yourself, in your way of thinking.

MARCUS AURELIUS

A rattlesnake, if cornered, will become so angry it will bite itself. That is exactly what the harboring of hate and resentment against others is—a biting of oneself. We think we are harming others, in holding these spites and hates, but the deeper harm is to ourselves.

E. STANLEY JONES

The best time for you to hold your tongue is the time you feel you must say something or bust.

JOSH BILLINGS

The height of human wisdom is to bring our tempers down to our circumstances and to make a calm within, under the weight of the greatest storm without.

DANIEL DEFOE

The greatest mistake you can make in life is to be continually fearing you will make one.

ELBERT HUBBARD

He is richest who is content with the least, for contentment is the wealth of nature.

SOCRATES

What is happiness other than the grace of being permitted to unfold to their fullest bloom all the spiritual powers planted within us.

FRANZ WERFEL

One sign of maturity is the ability to be comfortable with people who are not like us.

VIRGIL A. KRAFT

You probably wouldn't worry about what people think of you if you could know how seldom they do.

OLIN MILLER

Give me a good digestion, Lord,
   And also something to digest;
Give me a healthy body, Lord,
   With sense to keep it at its best;
Give me a healthy mind, good Lord,
   To keep the good and pure in sight
Which seeing sin is not appalled
   But finds a way to set it right;
Give me a mind that is not bored,
   That does not whimper, whine, or sigh;
Don't let me worry over much
   About a fussy thing called I.
Give me a sense of humour, Lord,
   Give me the grace to see a joke,
To get some happiness from life
   And pass it on to other folk.

PRAYER FOUND IN CHESTER CATHEDRAL

A THING OF BEAUTY

A thing of beauty is a joy for ever:
Its loveliness increases; it will never
Pass into nothingness; but still will keep
A bower quiet for us, and a sleep
Full of sweet dreams, and health, and quiet breathing.
Therefore, on every morrow, are we wreathing
A flowery band to bind us to the earth,
Spite of despondence, of the inhuman dearth
Of noble natures, of the gloomy days,
Of all the unhealthy and o'er-darkened ways
Made for our searching: yes, in spite of all,
Some shape of beauty moves away the pall
From our dark spirits. Such the sun, the moon,
Trees old and young, sprouting a shady boon
For simple sheep; and such are daffodils
With the green world they live in; and clear rills
That for themselves a cooling covert make
'Gainst the hot season; the mid-forest brake,
Rich with a sprinkling of fair musk-rose blooms:
And such too is the grandeur of the dooms
We have imagined for the mighty dead;
All lovely tales that we have heard or read:

An endless fountain of immortal drink,
Pouring unto us from the heaven's brink.
Nor do we merely feel these essences
For one short hour; no, even as the trees
That whisper round a temple become soon
Dear as the temple's self, so does the moon,
The passion poesy, glories infinite,
Haunt us till they become a cheering light
Unto our souls and bound to us so fast,
That, whether there be shine, or gloom o'ercast,
They always must be with us, or we die.

JOHN KEATS

PIED BEAUTY

Glory be to God for dappled things—
   For skies of couple-colour as a brinded cow;
      For rose-moles all in stipple upon trout that swim;
Fresh-firecoal chestnut-falls; finches' wings;
Landscape plotted and pieced—
       Fold, fallow, and plough;
      And all trades, their gear and tackle and trim.

All things counter, original, spare, strange;
    Whatever is fickle, freckled (who knows how?)
     With swift, slow; sweet, sour; adazzle, dim;
He fathers-forth whose beauty is past change:
    Praise Him.

GERARD MANLEY HOPKINS

Ideas are precious. An idea is the only lever which moves the world.
ARTHUR F. COREY

I have lived in this world just long enough to look carefully the second time into things that I was the most certain of the first time.
JOSH BILLINGS

A man should learn to detect and watch that gleam of light which flashes across his mind from within, more than the lustre of the firmament of bards and sages. Yet he dismisses without notice his thought, because it is his. In every work of genius we recognize our own rejected thoughts: they come back to us with a certain alienated majesty.
RALPH WALDO EMERSON

I respect faith, but doubt is what gets you an education.
WILSON MIZNER

Education would be much more effective if its purpose was to ensure that by the time they leave school every boy and girl should know how much they do *not* know, and be imbued with a lifelong desire to know it.
SIR WILLIAM HALEY

I Learn

No man has earned the right to intellectual ambition until he has learned to lay his course by a star which he has never seen—to dig by the divining rod for springs which he may never reach.

OLIVER WENDELL HOLMES, JR.

The aim of education should be to convert the mind into a living fountain, and not a reservoir. That which is filled by merely pumping in, will be emptied by pumping out.

JOHN M. MASON

The world does not pay for what a person knows. But it pays for what a person does with what he knows.

LAURENCE LEE

Education is an admirable thing, but it is well to remember from time to time that nothing that is worth knowing can be taught.

OSCAR WILDE

From the experience of others, do thou learn wisdom: and from their failings, correct thine own faults.

LORD CHESTERFIELD

We should be careful to get out of an experience only the wisdom that is in it—and stop there; lest we be like the cat that sits down on a hot stove lid. She will never sit down on a hot stove lid again—and that is well: but also she will never sit down on a cold one any more.

MARK TWAIN

I have learned to seek my happiness by limiting my desires, rather than in attempting to satisfy them.

JOHN STUART MILL

Life can only be understood backwards; but it must be lived forwards.
SØREN KIERKEGAARD

The trouble with most people is that they think with their hopes or fears or wishes rather than with their minds.
WALTER DURANTY

The aim of education should be to teach the child to think, not what to think.
JOHN DEWEY

Nothing is easier in America than to attend college, and nothing harder than to get educated.
DOUGLAS WOODRUFF

The classroom should be an entrance to the world, not an escape from it.
JOHN CIARDI

The scramble to get into college is so terrible these years that students are going to put up with almost anything, even an education.
BARNABY KEENEY

Courage is a special kind of knowledge: The knowledge of how to fear what ought to be feared and how not to fear what ought not to be feared.
DAVID BEN-GURION

A man who has committed a mistake and does not correct it is committing another mistake.
CONFUCIUS

ONCE A CHILD

It troubled me as once I was,
For I was once a child,
Deciding how an atom fell
And yet the heavens held.

The heavens weighed the most by far,
Yet blue and solid stood
Without a bolt that I could prove;
Would giants understand?

Life set me larger problems,
Some I shall keep to solve
Till algebra is easier
Or simpler proved above.

Then too be comprehended
What sorer puzzled me,
Why heaven did not break away
And tumble blue on me.
EMILY DICKINSON

A teacher who can arouse a feeling for one single
good action, for one single good poem, accomplishes
more than he who fills our memory with rows on rows
of natural objects, classified with name and form.
JOHANN WOLFGANG VON GOETHE

Reading is thinking with a strange head instead of
one's own.
ARTHUR SCHOPENHAUER

Blessed is the man who, having nothing to say,
abstains from giving in words evidence of the fact.
GEORGE ELIOT

The ability to speak several languages is an asset, but to be able to hold your tongue in one language is priceless.
SYDNEY SMITH

A fanatic is one who can't change his mind and won't change the subject.
WINSTON CHURCHILL

There is nothing so stupid as an educated man, if you get off the thing he was educated in.
WILL ROGERS

I have never let my schooling interfere with my education.
MARK TWAIN

Teach us that wealth is not elegance, that profusion is not magnificence, that splendor is not beauty.
BENJAMIN DISRAELI

Big doesn't necessarily mean better. Sunflowers aren't better than violets.
EDNA FERBER

It was Einstein who made the real trouble. He announced in 1905 that there was no such thing as absolute rest. After that there never was.
STEPHEN LEACOCK

Whether four years of strenuous attention to football and fraternities is the best preparation for professional work has never been seriously investigated.
ROBERT M. HUTCHINS

Valedictorian " . . . and this farewell would not be complete without expressing our debt of gratitude to a dedicated faculty. Oh, I know that it is the fashion to deprecate the value of personal contact as a valid part of education, and to say that a professor on tape or film is just as good as the real thing. But what course on film can offer the thrill of pulling the professor's lever and coming up with the right answer on the first try? What reel of tape can match the enthusiasm of even the newest instructor, fresh out of his factory carton? What canned pedagogy can equal the patience of the dedicated teacher whose relays will propound the same question over and over and over until it is correctly answered? No, we will never forget our mentors—L. C. Smith-Corona 607X, whose humanism enriched us all; or the winking dashboard of Remington Rand LV-44, when he would relieve the classroom tension by rolling up two lemons and a cherry; or the good sportsmanship of Univac 402 (transistor model) when we hid his fuse during Hell Week. These memories and more we take with us as we bid goodbye to our Alma Motor and face the challenge of . . . "

MARTIN LEVIN

The advantage of a classical education is that it enables you to despise the wealth which it prevents you from achieving.

RUSSELL GREEN

The best way I know of to win an argument is to start by being in the right.

LORD HAILSHAM

A great many people think they are thinking when they are merely rearranging their prejudices.
WILLIAM JAMES

PHYSICAL GEOGRAPHY

Sudden refreshment came upon the school
When in the tired afternoon we read
Of Rainfall, mountain ranges, watershed.
The whole United States stretched wide and cool.
Geography was dull; this other kind
With gulfs and glaciers, caves, and Rock Formation
In places of Products, People, Population,
Diffused a thrilling vapor through the mind.

There were three creatures—water, land and air—
Shifting so lightly yet with deep intent
Over the Country and the Continent,
Great creatures moving somber and aware,
Mixing and changing, making something new.
Theirs was the only work that never stops—
More interesting than Industries and Crops—
Creating clouds and sand and snow and dew.

And they could fashion terror when they listed:
New words like "funnel," "vortex," "spiral motion"
Explained the fearful Storms on Plains and Ocean.
Our dreams were sucked up violently and twisted,
The walls and blackboards slowly curved and spun,
There was a revolving speed, a rising core.
This room would not confine us as before
Since cyclones and tornadoes had begun.
LOUISE TOWNSEND NICHOLL

God, give me the courage to face a fact, though it slay me.
THOMAS HUXLEY

Books serve to show a man that those original thoughts of his aren't very new after all.
ABRAHAM LINCOLN

Reading is to the mind what exercise is to the body. As by the one health is preserved, strengthened, and invigorated; by the other, virtue, which is the health of the mind, is kept alive, cherished, and confirmed.
SIR RICHARD STEELE

That which you give most attention to grows quickest in life.
MAHARISHI MAHESH YOGI

It is much easier to be critical than to be correct.
BENJAMIN DISRAELI

Readers may be divided into four classes:
  1. Sponges, who absorb all they read and return it nearly in the same state, only a little dirtied.
  2. Sand-glasses, who retain nothing and are content to get through a book for the sake of getting through the time.
  3. Strain-bags, who retain merely the dregs of what they read.
  4. Mogul diamonds, equally rare and valuable, who profit by what they read, and enable others to profit by it also.
SAMUEL TAYLOR COLERIDGE

He who adds not to his learning diminishes it.
THE TALMUD

Education is the ability to listen to almost anything without losing your temper or your self-confidence.
ROBERT FROST

The test of a truly educated man is what he is, and what he thinks, and what his mind absorbs, or dreams, or creates, when he is alone.
DONALD K. DAVID

To profit from good advice requires more wisdom than to give it.
JOHN COLLINS

Advice is like snow, the softer it falls, the longer it dwells upon, and the deeper it sinks into, the mind.
SAMUEL TAYLOR COLERIDGE

The attempt to combine wisdom and power has only rarely been successful and then only for a short while.
ALBERT EINSTEIN

Human history becomes more and more a race between education and catastrophe.
H. G. WELLS

If you have knowledge, let others light their candles at it.
MARGARET FULLER

Common sense in an uncommon degree is what the world calls wisdom.
SAMUEL TAYLOR COLERIDGE

| ARITHMETIC

Arithmetic is where numbers fly like pigeons in and out of
your head.
Arithmetic tells you how many you lose or win if you
know how many you had before you lost or won.
Arithmetic is seven eleven all good children go to heaven
—or five six bundle of sticks.
Arithmetic is numbers you squeeze from your head to
your hand to your pencil to your paper till you get the
answer.
Arithmetic is where the answer is right and everything is
nice and you can look out of the window and see the
blue sky—or the answer is wrong and you have to start
all over and try again and see how it comes out this
time.

If you take a number and double it and double it again and
then double it a few more times, the number gets bigger
and bigger and goes higher and higher and only
arithmetic can tell you what the number is when you
decide to quit doubling.
Arithmetic is where you have to multiply—and you carry
the multiplication table in your head and hope you
won't lose it.
If you have two animal crackers, one good and one bad,
and you eat one and a striped zebra with streaks all over
him eats the other, how many animal crackers will you have
if somebody offers you five six seven and you say
No no no and you say Nay nay nay and you say Nix
nix nix?
If you ask your mother for one fried egg for breakfast and
she gives you two fried eggs and you eat both of them,
who is better in arithmetic, you or your mother?

CARL SANDBURG

| ## THE JOY OF DOING

We find greatest joy, not in getting, but in expressing what we are. There are tides in the ocean of life, and what comes in depends on what goes out. The currents flow inward only where there is an outlet. Nature does not give to those who will not spend; her gifts are loaned to those who will use them. Empty your lungs and breathe. Run, climb, work, and laugh; the more you give out, the more you shall receive. Be exhausted, and you shall be fed. Men do not really live for honors or for pay; their gladness is not in the taking and holding, but in the doing, the striving, the building, the living. It is a higher joy to teach than to be taught. It is good to get justice, but better to do it; fun to have things but more to make them. The happy man is he who lives the life of love, not for the honors it may bring, but for the life itself.

R. J. BAUGHAN

LIVING FOR OTHERS

The universe is everlasting.
The reason the universe is everlasting
   Is that it does not live for Self.
Therefore it can long endure.
Therefore the Sage puts himself last,
   And finds himself
     in the foremost place;
Regards his body as accidental,
   And his body is thereby
     preserved.
Is it not because he does not live for
   Self
That his Self achieves perfection?

LAO-TSE

| THE TIGER

Tiger! Tiger! burning bright
In the forests of the night,
What immortal hand or eye
Could frame thy fearful symmetry?

In what distant deeps or skies
Burnt the fire of thine eyes?
On what wings dare he aspire?
What the hand dare seize the fire?

And what shoulder, and what art,
Could twist the sinews of thy heart?
And when thy heart began to beat,
What dread hand? and what dread feet?

What the hammer? what the chain?
In what furnace was thy brain?
What the anvil? what dread grasp
Dare its deadly terrors clasp?

When the stars threw down their spears
And watered heaven with their tears,
Did he smile his work to see?
Did he who made the Lamb make thee?

Tiger! Tiger! burning bright
In the forests of the night,
What immortal hand or eye
Dare frame thy fearful symmetry?

WILLIAM BLAKE

The purpose of man's life is not happiness, but worthiness.

FELIX ADLER

To look up and not down,
To look forward and not back,
To look out and not in, and
To lend a hand.

EDWARD EVERETT HALE

Believe nothing merely because you have been told it, or it has been traditional, or because you yourselves have imagined it. Believe whatsoever you find to be conducive to the good, to benefit the welfare of all things.

BUDDHA

It is when we all play safe that we create a world of utmost insecurity.

DAG HAMMARSKJOLD

The world is now too dangerous for anything but the truth, too small for anything but brotherhood.

A. POWELL DAVIES

A split atom and a split mankind cannot co-exist indefinitely on the same planet.

LISTON POPE

I Care

There is an old Chinese saying that each generation builds a road for the next. The road has been well built for us, and I believe it incumbent upon us, in our generation, to build our road for the next generation.
JOHN F. KENNEDY

We should so live and labor in our time that what came to us as seed may go to the next generation as blossom, and what came to us as blossom may go to them as fruit. This is what we mean by progress.
HENRY WARD BEECHER

This country will not be a good place for any of us to live in unless we make it a good place for all of us to live in.
THEODORE ROOSEVELT

Join the great company of those who make the barren places of life fruitful with kindness. Carry a vision of heaven in your heart, and make the world correspond to that vision.
HELEN KELLER

Many times a day I realize how much my own life is built upon the labors of my fellowmen, and how earnestly I must exert myself in order to give in return as much as I have received.
ALBERT EINSTEIN

It is the art of mankind to polish the world, and everyone who works is scrubbing in some part.
HENRY DAVID THOREAU

It is a terrible, an inexorable, law that one cannot deny the humanity of another without diminishing one's own; in the face of the victim one sees oneself.
JAMES BALDWIN

Civilization is just a slow process of learning to be kind.
CHARLES L. LUCAS

If we could read the secret history of our enemies we should find in each man's life sorrow and suffering enough to disarm all hostility.
HENRY WADSWORTH LONGFELLOW

Justice will be achieved only when those who are not injured feel as indignant as those who are.
SOLON

The worst sin against our fellow creatures is not to hate them but to be indifferent to them.
GEORGE BERNARD SHAW

The real evil in the world is not the spectacular, the occasional, the vividly catastrophic. The real evil lies in our neglect of causes, our indifference to conditions, our unwillingness to give the time, the money and the effort to stop preventable disaster.
SYDNEY J. HARRIS

There is no escape—man drags man down, or man lifts man up.
BOOKER T. WASHINGTON

Human kindness has never weakened the stamina or softened the fiber of a free people. A nation does not have to be cruel in order to be tough.

FRANKLIN DELANO ROOSEVELT

If either man or woman would realize the full power of personal beauty, it must be by cherishing noble thoughts and hopes and purposes; by having something to do and something to live for that is worthy of humanity, and which, by expanding the capacities of the soul, gives expansion and symmetry to the body which contains it.

JAMES BAILEY UPHAM

It is the greatest of all mistakes to do nothing because you can only do a little. Do what you can.

SYDNEY SMITH

There are a thousand hacking at the branches of evil to one who is striking at the root.

HENRY DAVID THOREAU

When we understand each other, we find it difficult to cut one another's throats.

VAN WYCK BROOKS

Stop complaining about the management of the universe. Look around for a place to sow a few seeds of happiness.

HENRY VAN DYKE

One kind word can warm three winters.

JAPANESE PROVERB

If you treat an individual as he is, he will stay as he is: but if you treat him as if he were what he ought to be and could be, he will become what he ought to be and could be.

JOHANN WOLFGANG VON GOETHE

I am the inferior to any man whose rights I trample under foot.

RALPH INGERSOLL

You have not converted a man because you have silenced him.

JOHN MORLEY

He who cannot forgive breaks the bridge over which he himself must pass.

GEORGE HERBERT

Because we live within a stone's throw of each other is no reason why we should throw stones at each other.

STEPHEN S. WISE

A man has no more right to say an uncivil thing than to act one—no more right to say a rude thing to another man than to knock him down.

SAMUEL JOHNSON

A slander is like a hornet; if you cannot kill it dead at first blow, better not strike at all.

JOSH BILLINGS

One must be fond of people and trust them if one is not to make a mess of life.

E. M. FORSTER

I want it said of me that I always plucked a thistle and planted a flower, where I thought a flower would grow.
ABRAHAM LINCOLN

It takes so little to make people happy. Just a touch, if we know how to give it, just a word fitly spoken, a slight readjustment of some bolt or pin or bearing in the delicate machinery of a soul.
FRANK CRANE

If only men could be induced to laugh more they might hate less, and find more serenity here on earth.
MALCOLM MUGGERIDGE

Adapt yourself to the things among which your lot has been cast and love sincerely the fellow creatures with whom destiny has ordained that you shall live.
MARCUS AURELIUS

No soul is desolate as long as there is a human being for whom it can feel trust and reverence.
GAIUS GLENN ATKINS

No man has ever risen to the real stature of spiritual manhood until he has found that it is finer to serve somebody else than it is to serve himself.
WOODROW WILSON

Unless you find some sort of loyalty, you cannot find unity and peace in your active living.
JOSIAH ROYCE

To be happy is easy enough if we give ourselves, forgive others, and live with thanksgiving. Life is giving, not getting.
JOSEPH FORT NEWTON

A bone to the dog is not charity. Charity is the bone shared with the dog, when you are just as hungry as the dog.
JACK LONDON

It is people that count. You must put yourself into people; they touch others; these, others, and so you go on working for others forever.
ALICE FREEMAN PALMER

Persons are to be loved; things are to be used.
REUEL HOWE

The cheapest of all things is kindness, its exercise requiring the least possible trouble and self-sacrifice.
SAMUEL SMILES

Some fellows pay a compliment like they expected a receipt.
KIN HUBBARD

Do not offer a compliment and ask a favor at the same time. A compliment that is charged for is not valuable.
MARK TWAIN

Kindness means doing a lot of little things kindly and always; not just a big thing now and then.
NEVILLE HOBSON

Smile, for everyone lacks self-confidence . . . and more than any one thing a smile reassures them.
ANDRÉ MAUROIS

Forget injuries, never forget kindnesses.
CONFUCIUS

If men had no faith in each other, they would have to live within their incomes.

HERBERT V. PROCHNOW

The proper office of a friend is to side with you when you are in the wrong.

MARK TWAIN

LOYALTY

He may be six kinds of a liar,
  He may be ten kinds of a fool,
He may be a wicked highflyer
  Beyond any reason or rule;
There may be a shadow above him
  Of ruin and woes to impend,
And I may not respect, but I love him,
  Because—well, because he's my friend.

I know he has faults by the billion,
  But his faults are a portion of him;
I know that his record's vermilion
  And he's far from the sweet Seraphim;
But he's always been square with yours truly,
  Ready to give or to lend,
And if he is wild and unruly,
  I like him—because he's my friend.

I criticize him but I do it
  In just a frank, comradely key,
And back-biting gossips will rue it
  If ever *they* knock him to me!
I never make diagrams of him,
  No maps of his soul have I penned;
I don't analyze—I just love him,
  Because—well, because he's my friend.

BERTON BRALEY

| REMEMBRANCE

How many dear companions who enlivened for us
The world's rough road are gone, each fellow traveler
Much missed; yet say not sadly; they have left us!
But rather say, with gratitude: they were.

VASILY ZHUKOVSKY
translated by Babette Deutsch

If we would build on a sure foundation in friendship,
we must love our friends for their sakes rather than for
our own.

CHARLOTTE BRONTË

I love you
Because you have done
More than any creed
Could have done
To make me good,
And more than any fate
Could have done
To make me happy.

You have done it
Without a touch,
Without a word,
Without a sign.
You have done it
By being yourself,
Perhaps that is what
Being a friend means,
After all.

ROY CROFT

Instead of loving your enemies, treat your friends a little better.

E. H. HOWE

THE FRIEND WHO JUST STANDS BY

When trouble comes your soul to try,
You love the friend who just "stands by."
Perhaps there's nothing he can do—
The thing is strictly up to you;
For there are troubles all your own,
And paths the soul must tread alone;
Times when love cannot smooth the road
Nor friendship lift the heavy load,
But just to know you have a friend
Who will "stand by" until the end,
Whose sympathy through all endures,
Whose warm handclasp is always yours—
It helps someway, to pull you through,
Although there's nothing he can do.
And so with fervent heart you cry,
"God bless the friend who just 'stands by.' "

B. Y. WILLIAMS

Friendship is almost always the union of a part of one mind with a part of another; people are friends in spots.

GEORGE SANTAYANA

TO LOVE

To love is the most important thing in life. But what do we mean by love? When you love someone because that person loves you in return, surely that is not love. To love is to have that extraordinary feeling of affection without asking anything in return. . . . To love is the greatest thing in life; and it is very important to talk about love, to feel it, otherwise it is soon dissipated, for the world is very brutal. If while you are young you don't feel love, if you don't look with love at people, at animals, at flowers, when you grow up you will find that your life is empty; you will be very lonely, and the dark shadows of fear will follow you always. But the moment you have in your heart this extraordinary thing called love and feel the depth, the delight, the ecstasy of it, you will discover that for you the world is transformed.

J. KRISHNAMURTI

LOVE

Love is not primarily a relationship to a specific person; it is an attitude, an orientation of character which determines the relatedness of a person to the world as a whole, not toward one "object" of love. The active character of love becomes evident in the fact that it always implies certain basic elements, common to all forms of love. These are care, responsibility, respect and knowledge.
Love is the active concern for the life and the growth of that which we love.

ERICH FROMM

From THE HOUSE BY THE SIDE OF THE ROAD

'He was a friend to man, and lived
in a house by the side of the road.'—Homer

There are hermit souls that live withdrawn
In the peace of their self-content;
There are souls, like stars, that dwell apart,
In a fellowless firmament;
There are pioneer souls that blaze their paths
Where highways never ran;
But let me live by the side of the road
And be a friend to man.

Let me live in a house by the side of the road,
Where the race of men go by—
The men who are good and the men who are bad,
As good and as bad as I.
I would not sit in the scorner's seat,
Or hurl the cynic's ban;
Let me live in a house by the side of the road
And be a friend to man. . . .

SAM WALTER FOSS

| THE ROAD AND THE END

I shall foot it
Down the roadway in the dusk,
Where shapes of hunger wander
And the fugitives of pain go by.

I shall foot it
In the silence of the morning,
See the night slur into dawn,
Hear the slow great winds arise
Where tall trees flank the way
And shoulder toward the sky.

The broken boulders by the road
Shall not commemorate my ruin.
Regret shall be the gravel under foot.
I shall watch for
Slim swift of wing
That go where wind and ranks of thunder
Drive the wild processionals of rain.

The dust of the traveled road
Shall touch my hands and face.
CARL SANDBURG

If life were predictable it would cease to be life, and
be without flavor.
ELEANOR ROOSEVELT

I Am Free

Trust thyself; every heart vibrates to that iron string
. . . Who so would be a man, must be a nonconformist.
He who would gather immortal palms must not be
hindered by the name of goodness, but must explore if
it be goodness.
RALPH WALDO EMERSON

FOR POETS

Stay beautiful
but dont stay underground too long
Dont turn into a mole
or a worm
or a root
or a stone

Come in out into the sunlight
Breathe in trees
Knock out mountains
Commune with snakes
& be the very hero of birds
Dont forget to poke your head up
& blink
think
Walk all around
Swim upstream

Dont forget to fly
AL YOUNG

As human beings, we are endowed with freedom of
choice, and we cannot shuffle off our responsibility
upon the shoulders of God or nature. We must
shoulder it ourselves. It is up to us.
ARNOLD J. TOYNBEE

Life is not in abiding by fate, but rather in deciding one's fate.

PETER E. T. SEIFERT

Security is mostly a superstition. It does not exist in nature, nor do the children of men as a whole experience it. Avoiding danger is no safer in the long run than outright exposure. Life is either daring or nothing.

HELEN KELLER

To deny free will is to make mankind nothing but driftwood on the inexorable river of fate, and how we jostle one another is beyond our power to help.

J. A. MCWILLIAMS

Give me all the other advice you like, but don't tell me how to: bring up my children; train my dog; fish for trout; scramble eggs; cast my vote; select a football game; buy meat; eat lobster; appreciate good music; improve my disposition; relax; or prepare myself for heaven.

WILLIAM FEATHER

Last week I saw a man who had not made a mistake in 4,000 years. He was a mummy in the British Museum.

H. L. WAYLAND

A man must consider what a rich realm he abdicates when he becomes a conformist.

RALPH WALDO EMERSON

The first step which one makes in the world is the one on which depends the rest of our days.

VOLTAIRE

ADVENTURE

Sun and moon and beat of sea—
Great lands stretch endlessly.
Where be bonds to bind the free?
All the world was made for me!
ADELAIDE CRAPSEY

The most dangerous thing in the world is to try to leap a chasm in two jumps.
DAVID LLOYD GEORGE

We can't cross a bridge until we come to it; but I always like to lay down a pontoon ahead of time.
BERNARD M. BARUCH

The great pleasure in life is doing what people say you cannot do.
WALTER BAGEHOT

Thought takes man out of servitude, into freedom.
HENRY WADSWORTH LONGFELLOW

Freedom is more precious than any gifts for which you may be tempted to give it up.
BALTASAR GRACIAN

I know but one freedom and that is the freedom of the mind.
ANTOINE DE SAINT-EXUPÉRY

No man is free who is not a master of himself.
EPICTETUS

Afoot and light-hearted, I take to the
   open road,
Healthy, free, the world before me,
The long brown path before me, leading
   wherever I choose.

Henceforth I ask not good fortune—I
   myself am good-fortune;
Henceforth I whimper no more, postpone
   no more, need nothing,
Strong and content, I travel the open
   road . . .

WALT WHITMAN

Man's feet should be planted in his country, but his
eyes should survey the world.

GEORGE SANTAYANA

For this is what America is all about. It is the
uncrossed desert and the unclimbed ridge. It is the star
that is not reached and the harvest that's sleeping in
the unplowed ground.

LYNDON B. JOHNSON

No race can prosper till it learns that there is as much
dignity in tilling a field as in writing a poem.

BOOKER T. WASHINGTON

THE COLORS

You cannot choose your battlefield,
   The gods do that for you,
But you can plant a standard
   Where a standard never flew.

NATHALIA CRANE

Races didn't bother the Americans. They were something a lot better than any race. They were a People. They were the first self-constituted, self-declared, self-created People in the history of the world.

ARCHIBALD MACLEISH

Money and time are the heaviest burdens of life, and the unhappiest of all mortals are those who have more of either than they know how to use.

SAMUEL JOHNSON

He does not possess wealth that allows it to possess him.

BENJAMIN FRANKLIN

It is preoccupation with possessions, more than anything else, that prevents men from living freely and nobly.

BERTRAND RUSSELL

The flowers of all the tomorrows are in the seeds of today.

CHINESE PROVERB

Go confidently in the direction of your dreams! Live the life you've imagined! As you simplify your life, the laws of the universe will be simpler, solitude will not be solitude, poverty will not be poverty, nor weakness weakness.

HENRY DAVID THOREAU

Too many people are afraid of tomorrow—their happiness is poisoned by a phantom.

WILLIAM LYON PHELPS

Free will was granted to humanity. Man became conscious of good and evil, and his power of free choice. He acquired simultaneously Freedom and Responsibility. Henceforth he could help or he could hinder.

SIR OLIVER LODGE

I was part of that strange race of people aptly described as spending their lives doing things they detest to make money they don't want to buy things they don't need to impress people they dislike.

EMILE HENRY GAUVREAU

True progress consists not so much in increasing our needs as in diminishing our wants.

IVAN PANIN

Action and reaction, ebb and flow, trial and error, change—this is the rhythm of living. Out of our over-confidence, fear; out of our fear, clearer vision, fresh hope. And out of hope—progress.

BRUCE BARTON

Who bravely dares must sometimes risk a fall.

TOBIAS G. SMOLLETT

Our nation was built by men who took risks—pioneers who were not afraid of the wilderness; brave men who were not afraid of failure; scientists who were not afraid of truth; thinkers who were not afraid of progress; dreamers who were not afraid of action.

BROOKS ATKINSON

The crowning fortune of a man is to be born to some pursuit which finds him employment and happiness, whether it be to make baskets, or broadswords, or canals, or statues, or songs.

RALPH WALDO EMERSON

The reasonable man adapts himself to the world. The unreasonable one persists in trying to adapt the world to himself. Therefore all progress depends on the unreasonable man.

GEORGE BERNARD SHAW

You are not thrown to the winds, you
gather certainly and safely around
yourself.
Yourself! Yourself! yourself, for ever
and ever!

WALT WHITMAN

The surest way to corrupt a youth is to instruct him to hold in higher esteem those who think alike than those who think differently.

FRIEDRICH WILHELM NIETZSCHE

It is better to emit a scream in the shape of a theory than to be entirely insensible to the jars and incongruities of life and take everything as it comes in a forlorn stupidity. Some people swallow the universe like a pill; they travel on through the world, like smiling images pushed from behind. For God's sake give me the young man who has brains enough to make a fool of himself!

ROBERT LOUIS STEVENSON

| # HOLD FAST YOUR DREAMS

Hold fast your dreams!
Within your heart
Keep one still, secret spot
Where dreams may go,
And, sheltered so,
May thrive and grow
Where doubt and fear are not.
O keep a place apart,
Within your heart,
For little dreams to go!

Think still of lovely things that are not true.
Let wish and magic work at will in you.
Be sometimes blind to sorrow. Make believe!
Forget the calm that lies
In disillusioned eyes.
Though we all know that we must die,
Yet you and I
May walk like gods and be
Even now at home in immortality.

We see so many ugly things—
Deceits and wrongs and quarrelings;
We know, alas! we know
How quickly fade
The color in the west,
The bloom upon the flower,
The bloom upon the breast
And youth's blind hour.
Yet keep within your heart
A place apart
Where little dreams may go,
May thrive and grow.
Hold fast—hold fast your dreams!

LOUISE DRISCOLL

LINDBERGH FLIES ALONE

Alone?

Is he alone at whose right side rides
Courage, with Skill within the cockpit and
Faith upon the left? Does solitude surround
the brave when Adventure leads the way
and Ambition reads the dials? Is there no
company with him, for whom the air is cleft
by Daring and the darkness made light by
Emprise?

True, the fragile bodies of his fellows do
not weigh down his plane; true, the fretful
minds of weaker men are lacking from his
crowded cabin; but as his airship keeps
her course he holds communion with those
rare spirits that inspire to intrepidity and by
their sustaining potency give strength to
arm, resource to mind, content to soul.

Alone? With what other companions would
man fly to whom the choice were given?

An Editorial in the New York SUN, May 22, 1927.

71 | THE RESOLVE

To come to the river
the brook
hurtles through rainy
woods, over-
topping rocks that
before the rain were
islands.

Its clearness
is gone, and
the song.
It is a rich brown, a load
of churned earth
goes with it.

The sound now
is a direct, intense
sound of
direction.

DENISE LEVERTOV

Man, like the bridge, was designed to carry the load
of the moment, not the combined weight of a year at
once.

WILLIAM A. WARD

I Seek

'Tis the business of little minds to shrink; but he whose heart is firm, and whose conscience approves his conduct, will pursue his principles unto death.
THOMAS PAINE

That men have climbed the Matterhorn and McKinley means little. That they should *want* to climb them and *try* to climb them means everything. For it is the ultimate wisdom of the mountains that a man is never more a man than when he is striving for what is beyond his grasp, and that there is no conquest worth winning save that over his own weakness and fear.
JAMES RAMSEY ULLMAN

What am I, Life? A thing of watery salt
Held in cohesion by unresting cells,
Which work they know not why, which never halt,
Myself unwitting where their Master dwells.
I do not bid them, yet they toil, they spin;
A world which uses me as I use them,
Nor do I know which end or which begin
Nor which to praise, which pamper, which condemn.
So, like a marvel in a marvel set,
I answer to the vast, as wave by wave
The sea of air goes over, dry or wet,
Or the full moon comes swimming from her cave,
Or the great sun comes north, this myriad I
Tingles, not knowing how, yet wondering why.
JOHN MASEFIELD

Did you ever hear of a man who had striven all his life faithfully and singly toward an object and in no measure obtained it? Did ever a man try heroism, magnanimity, truth, sincerity, and find that there was no advantage in them, that it was a vain endeavor?
HENRY DAVID THOREAU

We lose much by fearing to attempt.
J. N. MAFFITT

Do not be too timid and squeamish about your
actions. All life is an experiment. The more
experiments you make the better. What if they are a
little coarse, and you may get your coat soiled or torn?
What if you do fail, and get fairly rolled in the dirt
once or twice? Up again; you shall never be so afraid
of a tumble.
RALPH WALDO EMERSON

There is a tide in the affairs of men
Which taken at the flood leads on to fortune;
Omitted, all the voyage of their life
Is bound in shallows and in miseries.
On such a full sea are we now afloat,
And we must take the current when it serves,
Or lose our ventures.
WILLIAM SHAKESPEARE

The men who try to do something and fail are
infinitely better than those who try to do nothing and
succeed.
LLOYD JONES

A man would do nothing if he waited until he could
do it so well that no one would find fault with what he
has done.
HENRY CARDINAL NEWMAN

It has always seemed to me that the most difficult part
of building a bridge would be the start.
ROBERT BENCHLEY

74

The reason a lot of people do not recognize an opportunity when they meet it is that it usually goes around wearing overalls and looking like hard work.
ANONYMOUS

It is no accomplishment in afterlife to be an ex-football player.
PAUL GALLICO

The man who removes a mountain begins by carrying away small stones.
CHINESE PROVERB

Thought is the seed of action.
RALPH WALDO EMERSON

Here is the secret of inspiration: Tell yourself that thousands and tens of thousands of people, not very intelligent and certainly no more intelligent than the rest of us, have mastered problems as difficult as those that now baffle you.
WILLIAM FEATHER

A map of the world that does not include Utopia is not worth glancing at.
OSCAR WILDE

Most men are so closely confined to the orbit of their worldly station that they have not even the courage to escape it by their ideas; and if there are some whom speculating on great matters unfits for small ones, there are yet more who by constant handling of small matters have lost the very sense of what is great.
MARQUIS DE VAUVENARGUES

I remember the gleams and glooms that dart
   Across the school-boy's brain;
The song and the silence in the heart
That in part are prophecies, and in part
   Are longings wild and vain.
     And the voice of that fitful song
     Sings on, and is never still:
     "A boy's will is the wind's will,
And the thoughts of youth are long, long thoughts."
HENRY WADSWORTH LONGFELLOW

Behind every advance of the human race is a germ of creation, growing in the mind of some lone individual. An individual whose dreams waken him in the night while others lie contentedly asleep.
CRAWFORD GREENEWALT

Ideals are like stars; you will not succeed in touching them with your hands. But, like the seafaring men on the desert of waters, you choose them as your guides, and following them reach your destiny.
CARL SCHURZ

It takes vision and courage to create—it takes faith and courage to prove.
OWEN D. YOUNG

We often discover what *will* do by finding out what will not do; and probably he who never made a mistake never made a discovery.
SAMUEL SMILES

In truth, people can generally make time for what they choose to do; it is not really the time but the will is lacking.

SIR JOHN LUBBOCK

MEASURE ME, SKY

Measure me, sky!
Tell me I reach by a song
Nearer the stars:
I have been little so long.

Weigh me, high wind!
What will your wild scales record?
Profit of pain,
Joy by the weight of a word.

Horizon, reach out!
Catch at my hands, stretch me taut,
Rim of the world:
Widen my eyes by a thought.

Sky, be my depth;
Wind, be my width and my height;
World, my heart's span:
Loneliness, wings for my flight!

LEONORA SPEYER

No great advance has ever been made in science, politics, or religion, without controversy.

LYMAN BEECHER

In the ordinary business of life, industry can do anything which genius can do, and very many things which it cannot.

HARRIET WARD BEECHER

Never stand begging for that which you have the power to earn.
MIGUEL DE CERVANTES

The first man gets the oyster, the second man gets the shell.
ANDREW CARNEGIE

Too often man handles life as he does the bad weather. He whiles away the time as he waits for it to stop.
ALFRED POLGAR

Things cannot always go your way. Learn to accept in silence the minor aggravations, cultivate the gift of taciturnity and consume your own smoke with an extra draught of hard work, so that those about you may not be annoyed with the dust and soot of your complaints.
EMMA LAZARUS

With me a change of trouble is as good as a vacation.
DAVID LLOYD GEORGE

What is the price of Experience? do men
   buy it for a song?
Or Wisdom for a dance in the street?
   No, it is bought with the price
Of all that a man hath, his house, his
   wife, his children.
Wisdom is sold in the desolate market
   where none come to buy,
And in the wither'd field where the
   farmer plows for bread in vain.
WILLIAM BLAKE

I have learned that success is to be measured not so much by the position that one has reached in life as by the obstacles which he has overcome while trying to succeed.

BOOKER T. WASHINGTON

If a man harbors any sort of fear, it percolates through all his thinking, damages his personality, makes him landlord to a ghost.

LLOYD C. DOUGLAS

Do not attempt to do a thing unless you are sure of yourself; but do not relinquish it because someone else is not sure of you.

STEWART E. WHITE

The happiness of your life depends upon the quality of your thoughts, therefore guard accordingly; and take care that you entertain no notions unsuitable to virtue and reasonable nature.

MARCUS ANTONINUS

There is a pleasure in the pathless woods,
There is a rapture on the lonely shore,
There is society where none intrudes,
By the deep sea, and music in its roar:
I love not man the less, but Nature more,
From these our interviews, in which I steal
From all I may be, or have been before,
To mingle with the universe and feel
What I can ne'er express, yet cannot all
   conceal.

GEORGE GORDON, LORD BYRON

Happiness is everywhere, and its spring is in our own heart.

JOHN RUSKIN

Far away there in the sunshine are my highest aspirations. I may not reach them, but I can look up and see their beauty, believe in them, and try to follow where they lead.

LOUISA MAY ALCOTT

Where there seems no way to go
go anyway
don't be put off by what you can't see
get up any which way
scramble on hands and knees
ditching your pride
slide along the bottom for a stretch
clutch at roots
and keep going on

once up there you can look back to
the pathway you have cleared
that will make it easier
next time you climb.

EVE MERRIAM

Strengthen me by sympathizing with my strength not my weakness.

AMOS BRONSON ALCOTT

A strength is merely a weakness put to good advantage.

GARY B. WRIGHT

The block of granite which is an obstacle in the pathway of the weak, becomes a stepping-stone in the pathway of the strong.
THOMAS CARLYLE

It may be that the race is not always to the swift, not the battle to the strong—but that is the way to bet.
DAMON RUNYON

We may take Fancy for a companion, but must follow Reason as our guide.
SAMUEL JOHNSON

Farming looks mighty easy when your plow is a pencil, and you're a thousand miles from the corn field.
DWIGHT EISENHOWER

Make your life a happy one. That is where success is possible to every man.
SIR ROBERT STEPHENSON SMYTH BADEN-POWELL

If we are ever to enjoy life, now is the time—not tomorrow, nor next year, nor in some future life after we have died. The best preparation for a better life next year is a full, complete, harmonious, joyous life this year.
THOMAS DREIER

A sense of the value of time—that is, of the best way to divide one's time into one's various activities—is an essential preliminary to efficient work; it is the only method of avoiding hurry.
ARNOLD BENNETT

RELATIVITY

There was a young lady named Bright,
Who traveled much faster than light.
    She started one day
    In the relative way,
And returned on the previous night.
ANONYMOUS

Weep not that the world changes—did it keep a
stable, changeless state, it were a cause indeed to
weep.
WILLIAM CULLEN BRYANT

There is a certain relief in change, even though it be
from bad to worse; as I have found in traveling in a
stage-coach, that it is often a comfort to shift one's
position and be bruised in a new place.
WASHINGTON IRVING

Ah, what a dusty answer gets the soul when hot for
certainties in this our life!
GEORGE MEREDITH

People are always blaming their circumstances for
what they are. I don't believe in circumstances. The
people who get on in this world are the people who get
up and look for the circumstances they want, and if
they can't find them, make them.
GEORGE BERNARD SHAW

If you don't get everything you want, think of the
things you don't get that you don't want.
OSCAR WILDE

Most people live, whether physically, intellectually or morally, in a very restricted circle of their potential being. They *make use* of a very small portion of their possible consciousness, and of their soul's resources in general, much like a man who, out of his whole bodily organism, should get into a habit of using and moving only his little finger. Great emergencies and crises show us how much greater our vital resources are than we had supposed.

WILLIAM JAMES

The business of life is to go forwards.

SAMUEL JOHNSON

Ambition is so powerful a passion in the human breast, that however high we reach we are never satisfied.

NICCOLÓ MACHIAVELLI

Experience shows that success is due less to ability than to zeal. The winner is he who gives himself to his work, body and soul.

CHARLES BUXTON

If A equal success, then the formula is A equals X plus Y and Z, with X being work, Y play, and Z keeping your mouth shut.

ALBERT EINSTEIN

Far better it is to dare mighty things, to win glorious triumphs, even though checkered by failure, than to rank with those poor spirits who neither enjoy much nor suffer much, because they live in the gray twilight that knows not victory nor defeat.

THEODORE ROOSEVELT

| ## THE BUILDERS

All are architects of Fate,
    Working in these walls of Time;
Some with massive deeds and great,
    Some with ornaments of rhyme.

Nothing useless is, or low;
    Each thing in its place is best;
And what seems but idle show
    Strengthens and supports the rest.

For the structure that we raise,
    Time is with materials filled;
Our todays and yesterdays
    Are the blocks with which we build.

Truly shape and fashion these;
    Leave no yawning gaps between;
Think not, because no man sees,
    Such things will remain unseen.

In the elder days of Art,
    Builders wrought with greatest care
Each minute and unseen part;
    For the gods see everywhere.

Let us do our work as well.
    Both the unseen and the seen;
Make the house where gods may dwell
    Beautiful, entire, and clean.

Else our lives are incomplete,
    Standing in these walls of Time,
Broken stairways, where the feet
    Stumble, as they seek to climb.

Build today, then, strong and sure,
    With a firm and ample base;
And ascending and secure
    Shall tomorrow find its place.

Thus alone can we attain
    To those turrets, where the eye
Sees the world as one vast plain,
    And one boundless reach of sky.

HENRY WADSWORTH LONGFELLOW

Last, but by no means least, courage—moral courage,
the courage of one's convictions, the courage to see
things through. The world is in a constant conspiracy
against the brave. It's the age-old struggle—the roar of
the crowd on one side and the voice of your conscience
on the other.

DOUGLAS MACARTHUR

May the road rise to meet you.
May the wind be ever at your back
May the Good Lord keep you in the
   hollow of His hand.
May your heart be as warm as your
   hearthstone.
May God bless you always.

OLD IRISH BLESSING

These, then, are my last words to you: Be not afraid of
life. Believe that life is worth living and your belief will
help create the fact.

WILLIAM JAMES

ACKNOWLEDGMENTS

The editor and the publisher have made every effort to trace the ownership of all copyrighted material and to secure permission from copyright holders of such material. In the event of any question arising as to the use of any material the publisher and editor, while expressing regret for inadvertent error, will be pleased to make the necessary corrections in future printings. Thanks are due to the following authors, publishers, publications and agents for permission to use the material indicated.

ATHENEUM PUBLISHERS, INC., for "Finding a Poem #2," from *Finding a Poem* by Eve Merriam, copyright © 1970 by Eve Merriam.

BABETTE DEUTSCH, for "Remembrance" by Vasily Zhukovsky, from *Two Centuries of Russian Verse, from Lomonosov to Voznesenky,* edited, with an Introduction and Notes, by Avrahm Yarmolinsky; translations by Babette Deutsch.

E. P. DUTTON & CO. INC., for "Physical Geography" from *Collected Poems* by Louise Townsend Nicholl, copyright 1953 by E. P. Dutton & Co. Inc.

BERNICE WILLIAMS FOLEY, for "The Friend Who Just Stands By," by B. Y. Williams.

MRS. ARTHUR GUITERMAN, for selection from *Death and General Putnam* by Arthur Guiterman, copyright renewed by Vida Lindo Guiterman.

SYDNEY J. HARRIS and Field NEWSPAPER SYNDICATE for excerpt.

HARCOURT BRACE JOVANOVICH, INC., for "Arithmetic" from *Complete Poems* by Carl Sandburg, copyright 1950 by Carl Sandburg; for "The Road and the End" from *Chicago Poems* by Carl Sandburg, copyright 1916 by Holt, Rinehart and Winston, Inc., copyright 1944 by Carl Sandburg.

HARPER & ROW, PUBLISHERS, INC., for excerpts from *The Art of Loving* by Erich Fromm, Volume Nine of the World Perspective Series edited by Ruth Nanda Anshen, copyright © 1956 by Erich Fromm; for excerpt from the Foreword to *Conquest by Man* by Paul Herrmann, translated from the German by Michael Bullock, copyright 1954 by Harper & Row, Publishers, Inc.; for "To Love," from *Think on These Things* by J. Krishnamurti, copyright 1964 by Krishnamurti Writings, Inc.

HARVARD UNIVERSITY PRESS, for Poem #600 "It troubled me as once I was," from *The Poems of Emily Dickinson,* edited by Thomas H. Johnson; reprinted by permission of the Publishers and the Trustees of Amherst College, the Belknap Press of Harvard University Press; copyright © 1951, 1955 by the President and Fellows of Harvard College.

ALFRED A. KNOPF, INC., for "Poem" from *The Dream Keeper and Other Poems* by Langston Hughes, copyright 1932 and renewed 1960 by Langston Hughes; for "Hope" from *Selected Poems* by Langston Hughes, copyright 1942 by Alfred A. Knopf, Inc., renewed 1970 by Arna Bontemps and George Houston Bass; for "Measure Me, Sky," from *Slow Wall. Poems together with or Without Music and Further Poems,* by Leonora Speyer, renewed 1967 by the Estate of Leonora Speyer.

MARTIN LEVIN for "Valedictory 2065" from *The Phoenix's Nest.*

MACMILLAN PUBLISHING CO. INC., for "What Am I, Life," from *Poems* by John Masefield, copyright 1916, renewed 1964 by John Masefield; for "The High School Band," from *The Self-Made Man and other Poems* by Reed Whittemore, copyright © 1959 by Reed Whittemore.

MRS. VIRGIL MARKHAM, for selection by Edwin Markham.

NEW DIRECTIONS PUBLISHING CORP., for "The Resolve" from *O Taste and See* by Denise Levertov, copyright © 1964 by Denise Levertov Goodman.

CHARLES SCRIBNER'S SONS for "Who Am I" from *At the Top of My Voice* by Felice Holman, copyright © 1970 by Felice Holman.

SIMON & SCHUSTER, INC., for excerpt from *The Business of Life* by William Feather.

THE SOCIETY OF AUTHORS for excerpts from the plays of Bernard Shaw.

MAY SWENSON, for "After the Dentist" from *Half Sun Half Sleep,* copyright © 1967 by May Swenson.

FELICE HOLMAN VALEN, for "Who Am I" from *At the Top of My Voice,* copyright © 1970 by Felice Holman.

A. P. WATT & SON, on behalf of Mrs. Dorothy Cheston Bennett, for selection by Arnold Bennett.

YALE UNIVERSITY PRESS, for "Days" from *Blue Smoke* by Karle Wilson Baker.

Set in Elegante
—phototype version of Palatino, roman and italic.

Designed by Ladislav Svatos.

Photographs by Peter Tepper.